Mrs Stevens
41 years old

Granma
70 years old

Laura
12 years old

Mr Stevens
43 years old

Dexter
8 years old

Martin
16 years old

CIVIL RIGHTS... IN THE USA

by
Maureen Montgomery

Macdonald Educational

What is this book about?

This book is about civil rights. These are the rights of all citizens to be treated equally in important areas of life: housing, voting, education and jobs. In particular it is about the struggle that black Americans have fought, and are still fighting, to be respected as the equals of white people in the USA.

How to use this book

Laura is a black girl living in Atlanta today. Part of this book tells the story of Laura's family. But the photographs in the parts of the book marked 'Evidence' and 'Comment' are of real people. They tell the history of the struggle of black Americans, and other minority groups, to be treated fairly and equally. Use this book to find out how life has changed for black people, and see what still needs to be done to achieve equal rights for all minority groups.

Factual Adviser
Professor Thomas L. Blair
School of Environmental Studies
Polytechnic of Central London

Educational Adviser
Alistair Ross
Principal Lecturer in Primary Education
Polytechnic of North London

Series Editor Nicole Lagneau

Book Editor Stephen White-Thomson

Teacher Panel
Stewart Ross, Tim Firth, Jeffrey Reid

Design Sally Boothroyd

Production Rosemary Bishop

Picture Research Diana Morris

A MACDONALD BOOK

© Macdonald & Company (Publishers) Ltd 1986

First published in Great Britain in 1986 by Macdonald & Company (Publishers) Ltd, London & Sydney
A BPCC plc company
All rights reserved

Printed and bound in Great Britain by Purnell Book Production Ltd, Paulton, nr. Bristol

Macdonald & Co (Publishers) Ltd
Maxwell House
74, Worship Street
London EC2A 2EN

British Library Cataloguing in Publication Data
Montgomery, Maureen
    Civil rights in the USA.——(People then and now; 4)
    1. Civil rights——United States
    I. Title   II. Series
    323.4'0973   JC599.US
    ISBN 0-356-11229-2

Contents

Laura's new friend

There was a knock at the door. 'Come in!' called Mrs Evans, Laura's maths teacher. A girl poked her head around the door. Everyone stopped their work and stared. The new girl stood in the doorway, looking at her feet. She was wearing a grey skirt, jumper and tie. Laura didn't know any girls who wore ties and uniforms to school.

'Okay, you can stop working for a moment,' said Mrs Evans to the class. 'I'd like to introduce you to your new classmate, Helen Fraser, from England. Her family have come to live in Atlanta, and she will be joining our class. Laura Stevens,' Mrs Evans continued, 'I'd like you to look after Helen for a few days and show her around the neighbourhood. Helen, will you come and collect some maths books from the cupboard, and then we can all get back to work.'

When the bell went for lunch, Laura took Helen out into the school yard. They sat under a tree and took out their lunch-boxes. 'Why are you wearing a tie?' asked Laura. Helen went red. 'Umm. My mother made me put on my old school uniform. I feel really silly.' 'We are lucky,' said Laura. 'We never have to wear uniforms to school. We just wear the same kind of clothes we wear at home. It's so much more comfortable.'

Laura opened her lunch-box. 'Where do these kids come from?' asked Helen, looking around. 'They don't look American to me.' 'It depends what you think Americans look like,' said Laura. 'People from all over the world have come to live in America.

Take George, his mum is Japanese. And Tony over there – his parents come from Mexico.' 'I didn't know there was such a mixture of people here,' said Helen.

They were munching their sandwiches when Helen suddenly asked, 'What on earth is that in your sandwiches?' 'This? It's just peanut butter and jelly,' replied Laura, a little puzzled. 'Jelly!' said Helen. 'Yes! Here, have a bite,' said Laura, offering Helen a sandwich. 'Oh! It's jam!' said Helen. 'What a strange mixture. I've never had that before.' 'You don't know what you're missing!' smiled Laura, tucking into her lunch.

8

Atlanta is the capital of the Southern state of Georgia, see map on page 11. In 1864 it was captured by Union troops during the Civil War (1861–1865). ▼

Today, the modern city of Atlanta is the headquarters for the civil rights movement. ▶

◀ In 1963, civil rights leader, Martin Luther King, told a huge crowd in America's capital, Washington DC, of his dream that, one day, all American people would be treated equally.

Stone Mountain

'How about a drive into the country?' asked Laura's Dad, Mr Stevens. 'It's nice and sunny and you shouldn't be stuck indoors all day.' It was Sunday afternoon. Helen, Laura and Dexter, Laura's eight-year-old brother, were lounging around, watching television and drinking soda.

A few minutes later, Mr and Mrs Stevens, Laura, Dexter and Helen bundled into the car. They drove through the wide streets of Atlanta. Soon they were driving past Stone Mountain. Suddenly, Dexter cried out, 'Look over there!' He pointed to a carving high up on the side of the mountain. 'Who are those men on horses?' 'That's Jefferson Davis and his generals,' his mother told him.

Mr Stevens stopped the car in a lay-by. 'Let's all get out and have a closer look. If you're very lucky, you might even see some squirrels.' Helen looked over the treetops towards the carving. 'Who is Jefferson Davis?' she asked.

'Let me give you some background! More than a hundred years ago, Americans fought a war against other Americans,' Mr Stevens explained. 'The Southern states decided to break away from the Union which had kept all the American states together. Jefferson Davis was the President of the Southern states. The South wanted to form a separate country. It was tired of being told what to do by people in the North. You see, some Northerners were trying to make Southern shareholders free their black slaves. The Southerners didn't want to do that.'

'What happened then?' asked Dexter. 'In short, the North and South went to war and the South was defeated,' said Mr Stevens. 'Were the slaves freed?' asked Helen. 'Yes, they were, but some Southern whites did not accept the ex-slaves as their equals. They tried to frighten black people in the South to show them that they were still the bosses. They burned down barns and houses.'

'I've seen pictures of that in books at school. They look really spooky,' said Laura. 'Were they the Klan?' 'Yes, that's right,' replied her mother, 'and it was on this mountain that the Klan was started up again in 1915. The Klan had died out for a while, but they started their campaign of violence again during the troubled times of the World War One years. You still see them from time to time, parading in towns. They want to remind us that there are some white people who think that black people don't belong in America.' Laura's mother sighed, and then blurted out. 'Hey, we're in luck. Here's a squirrel for you to play with!'

Members of the Ku Klux Klan hold secret meetings at night. They are an illegal organization that started in the 1860s. They believe that blacks are inferior to whites.

EVIDENCE

This American wears the Nazi symbol, the swastika. Like the Nazis, he believes that whites are better than blacks. ▼

THE TERRITORIES

Atlanta

▨	Free states
☐	Slave states within the Union
▨	Confederate states
—	Division between Union and Confederacy

America in the Civil War, (1861–1865). Name the states by looking them up in an atlas.

Civil rights

For many years, black Americans were not allowed to use the same seats on buses or the same toilets or drinking fountains as whites. They had to eat in separate restaurants and shop in separate shops. This was known as segregation.

The greatest opposition to segregation came in the 1950s and 1960s. During these years, groups were organized by people like the Reverend Martin Luther King to protest peacefully against the unfair treatment of black Americans. Black Americans demanded equality. They wanted to have the same rights to jobs, housing, voting and education as their fellow white Americans. These rights are called civil rights. In 1963 nearly a quarter of a million people marched to the capital of the USA, Washington DC, and heard Martin Luther King speak out against inequality.

Some blacks looked for other, less peaceful, ways of protesting against inequality. They rejected the help of whites and wanted all black people to help one another and work together. They were proud of being black. They demanded their rights – and some of them were prepared to use violence to get them. Their slogan was 'Black Power'.

This man brings up his child to believe that blacks must struggle to be treated equally.

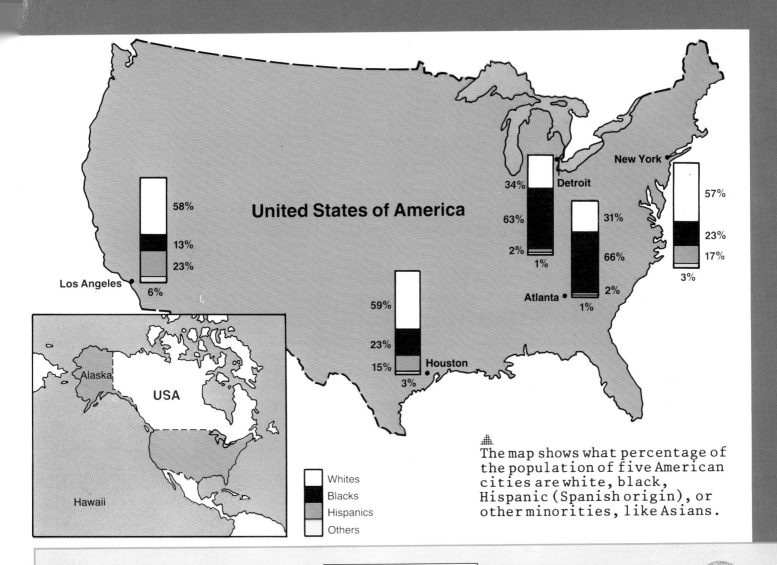

United States of America

Los Angeles
- 58% Whites
- 13% Blacks
- 23% Hispanics
- 6% Others

Detroit
- 34%
- 63%
- 2%
- 1%

Atlanta
- 31%
- 66%
- 2%
- 1%

New York
- 57%
- 23%
- 17%
- 3%

Houston
- 59%
- 23%
- 15%
- 3%

USA
Alaska
Hawaii

Legend:
- Whites
- Blacks
- Hispanics
- Others

The map shows what percentage of the population of five American cities are white, black, Hispanic (Spanish origin), or other minorities, like Asians.

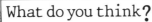

What do you think?

Until 1964 it was legal in the Southern United States to display signs saying 'Colored Only' or 'Whites Only' at cinemas and on drinking fountains and toilets. The trouble was that the places for black people were never as smart as the places for white people.

How would you like to be told that you have to walk a kilometre to another shop, when you are passing a shop that sells what you want, but you cannot go into it because your skin is the wrong colour? Should the colour of your skin make any difference to where you can shop, where you sit on a bus, or where you eat in town?

Going to school

'As it's the 25th anniversary of our school this year,' Mrs Evans announced, 'we are going to do a history project on schools in America.' It was Monday afternoon and Laura's class was having a history lesson. There were loud groans from Laura and her classmates. Projects were hard work. 'There will be a prize for the best project,' added Mrs Evans. 'The mayor of Atlanta will present the winner with a book of his or her choice at the end of term.'

'What do we have to do, Mrs Evans?' Laura asked. 'Well, first, I'm going to tell you a little about the history of schools in America and then you can decide what kind of school you want to write about. Schools have played an important part in our history. The ideas people have had over the years about what things should be taught, and who schools were for, tell us a lot about the country we live in.'

'I'd like to do Indian schools on the reservations,' said Helen, as she and Laura walked home from the bus-stop later that day. 'American Indians have had a bad time, haven't they?' 'Yes,' Laura agreed. 'They were the first people to live in America. Over the last 200 years, they have lost most of the land that was once theirs.' 'It's very unfair,' said Helen. 'Yes, it is.' Laura nodded. 'But it will be an interesting project. And I can help you because I did a project on the American West last year.'

'Thanks, Laura. That'll be great.' 'I'm going to see if my mum can help me with my project,' said Laura.

'She's a teacher. Perhaps I could do something on her schooldays. I remember her saying that she was taken to school by troops once, when they first started to let black children go to white schools.'

'Did black children go to different schools from white kids then?' asked Helen. 'Yes. My mum told me. She used to go to an all-black school at first and then she went to a high school where nearly all the kids were white. She hated it because she was teased for being black. But she still believes that black and white children should go to school together.' 'That sounds really interesting,' said Helen. 'It will make a good project.'

These children are saluting the American flag in a New York school at the end of the nineteenth century. American children do the same today. Many of the children in the picture had parents who were born in Europe.

EVIDENCE

In some areas of the United States, there is the danger of violence between blacks and whites. To prevent violence from breaking out in inner-city schools, like this one, police patrol the grounds and the buildings. The fences around some schools are made of barbed wire.

'Yes, and it fits in with what Mrs Evans was saying about equality and education,' said Laura. 'You know, the bit about people wanting every child to have an equal chance. When they began to mix the schools they said it would help to make sure that blacks were treated as equals to whites. They said if blacks and whites went to school together, they would learn to live with each other.'

'I hope that's true,' said Helen. 'This is my turning. I'll see you tomorrow.' 'Bye!' called Laura as she started to run home. Her mother had an old photo album from her schooldays and Laura had an idea about what she wanted to do.

Mum's schooldays

In September 1957 the Central High School at Little Rock in Arkansas began to admit black students. Local whites protested violently, and shouted insults at the black students as they tried to enter the school. ⏵

'Laura! I hope you are going to put all those things back in that drawer. What are you looking for?' 'I will, Mum. I can't find that album of yours with pictures of you at school.' Laura's mother put down the pile of exercise books she was carrying and took out the album Laura was hunting for, from another drawer. 'Oh great!' cried Laura. 'Just a minute,' said her mother. 'You haven't told me what you want it for.'

'I've got another history project to do,' Laura explained. 'This time we've got to choose a period in history and write about what kinds of school there were. We can pick a school for immigrants, or a colonial school, or a frontier school.' 'And what are you doing?' asked Mrs Stevens.

'Well, I thought I could write about the school you went to, Mum. You know, where there was all that trouble about mixing blacks and whites together, so that they could have the same chances in life. What's the long word for that?' 'Integration,' Mrs Stevens replied.

'Yes, that's it! I remember you telling cousin Patty about it at Christmas. You said your picture was in the newspaper because you were one of the first black kids to go to a white school.' 'I see,' said her mother. 'And are you going to write about what happened in the 1960s when they tried to mix the schools, based on what happened to me?'

'Yes,' said Laura. 'I thought it would be a good idea to get hold of that newspaper clipping.

Governor Wallace of Alabama was once fiercely opposed to letting black Americans go to all-white colleges. In 1963 he blocked the entrance of two black students into the University of Alabama. ▶

Then I could interview you about how you felt going to that school with the white people shouting and protesting against opening the schools to children of all races. It must have been scary.'

'Well a lot of things were happening in the South at that time,' Mrs Stevens sighed. 'Things died down eventually. People slowly got used to the idea of integrated schools. But, even now, you have schools with only black or only white children. Things are still not perfect.'

'I'll go through your album, Mum, and use some of the pictures, if that's okay.' 'Yes, dear, that's fine. But look after them. They're part of my history!'

One way round the problem of segregated schools was to bus black children out of the inner cities to schools in the white suburbs. This upset some black and white parents and there was much opposition to busing. Busing is still not popular today.

Education

In the Southern states there were no schools for black children until after the Civil War ended in 1865. Even then, black children had to go to separate schools from whites. In 1896 the Supreme Court, the most important court in America, said it was fair for black children to go to separate schools, providing the schools were of the same standard as white schools. But, in fact, they were never equal.

Civil rights groups tried to prove to the Supreme Court that separate schools provided for black children were worse than schools for white children.

In 1954, after a long struggle, the Supreme Court was persuaded to change its mind. It stated that blacks and whites should be educated together in the same schools.

But many white Americans were strongly opposed to mixing black and white children in schools. Their protests were sometimes so violent that schools were closed. Today, it is still difficult to integrate schools in big cities. To try and make things better, children are bussed from a black ghetto area to a school in a white suburb. But this is sometimes unpopular with both whites and blacks, and so the problem remains.

All-white schools like this can no longer refuse a place to a black pupil.

For many years after slavery was ended in 1863, there was little effort made in the South to provide schools and properly-trained teachers for black children. Most black schools had one room where all the children were taught together. Often, there were no school books for the children to work from. Some schools still have too few books for their students.

What do you think?

Today, many children of all races attend integrated (mixed) schools in the USA. Schools are important places for children of all races and colours to mix together and learn about each other. How else can we learn to live together in peace unless we get to know, and trust, each other?

A lazy afternoon

'What are you wearing to Julie's party tomorrow?' asked Helen. She and Laura had been invited to the birthday party of one of their classmates. 'Open the wardrobe behind you. Do you see the pink outfit? Yes, that's it,' said Laura. 'Oh, this is really nice,' said Helen as she took it out of the wardrobe, and laid it carefully on the bed.

'I'm going to get Mum to braid my hair and thread beads on it. She doesn't do it very often because it takes such a long time. She doesn't really like it – she keeps saying I'll go bald!' 'Stevie Wonder has his hair braided, doesn't he?' asked Helen. 'Yes, he does. Do you like his music, Helen? My mum likes him a lot. She likes the words to his songs. He often sings about being black and how blacks and whites should live together in harmony.'

'Is it weird having crinkly hair?' Helen asked, looking at Laura who was combing her hair with an 'Afro' comb. 'Not at all. You're weird having straight hair!' Laura teased. 'Try combing my hair!'

'What are you giving Julie for her birthday?' asked Helen. 'A poster of Michael Jackson. I found a really big one. She's crazy about him. Is he really well-known in England?' 'I'll say!' said Helen. 'He's really made it big in America. He's ever so rich. Do you get a lot of American music in Britain?' 'I suppose so,' answered Helen. 'But I don't always know if the groups are British or American!'

'Have you heard any Motown music?' asked Laura. 'What's that?' 'I'll play some for you,' said Laura.

She took a record out of its sleeve and put it on her record player. 'It's black music. Motown was a black record company in Detroit. Motown is short for Motortown because they build so many cars in Detroit and a lot of black people work in the car factories.'

'What's black music, Laura?' 'Well, I suppose it's music that's written and performed by blacks. Black music has its roots in African music and slave spirituals and things like that. The beat is quite different. Black music can be really sad, like the blues. Black people have had a lot to be sad about over the years.'

'I hope they play music like this at the party,' said Helen excitedly, dancing about. 'It's really good to dance to.' 'Ouch! Careful what you're doing to my hair!' cried Laura.

Louis 'Satchmo'
(Satchel-mouth)
Armstrong [1900-1971]
was one of the most
famous jazz trumpeters
of all time.

Stevie Wonder is a
world-famous singer.
He led the campaign to
have the birthday of
Martin Luther King
(15 January) made a
national holiday. ▼

EVIDENCE

White entertainers, like Al
Jolson, used to 'black up'
before doing their singing
and dancing acts to portray
blacks as simple-minded.

Martin's big game

'Has everyone got popcorn?' asked Mr Stevens. 'Are you okay, Dex?' Dexter tried to answer, but he couldn't. His mouth was too full of food. Hundreds of people were queueing outside the school to see the big basketball game. Martin, Laura's 16-year-old brother, was playing for his high-school team. This was an important match for him. He wanted to play basketball when he went to college and be as successful as his hero, Patrick Ewing, who played for a famous New York team.

Helen had never been to a basketball game before and she was amazed at the crowds and how serious everyone was about the game.

'Oh look!' cried Dexter. 'I can see Martin!' He looks very nervous,' said his mother. Martin was bouncing a ball, waiting for the teams to be called. There were cheerleaders for both teams, swinging pom-poms and chanting, 'Two, four, six, eight, who do we appreciate? WARNER HIGH!'

The teams came on to the court to start the game. It was a fast, evenly-matched game. Mr Stevens bounced up and down in his seat with excitement. 'Go for it, Martin!' he yelled. Martin started shakily at first. It took some time for him to settle down. Then from somewhere he found a magic touch and scored every time he aimed at the basket.

It was coming up to the last minute, and the score was 68-all. The opposing team had the ball. The seconds were running out. Martin leapt up high to catch the ball. He raced down, dribbling past several defenders to his goal. Mrs Stevens shut her eyes. She couldn't bear to look. Then there was a huge cheer. 'Did he score?' she asked anxiously. 'Of course! We've won!' yelled Laura. Everyone was out of their seats, yelling and shouting.

As Martin came out of the changing rooms, his father said to him: 'Well, son, Patrick Ewing has got nothing on you!' 'Come on, Dad,' said Martin, 'I've got a long way to go yet!' 'I'll get you an ice cream' said Mr Stevens. 'Hands up all those who want to go to Finkel's Ice Cream Parlour!'

Muhammad Ali, World
Heavyweight Boxing
Champion, 1964-1970
and 1974-1978, has
always spoken out
against racism.

Few black tennis
players have made it to
the top, but, in 1985,
Zena Garrison was a
quarter-finalist at
the Wimbledon
Championships. ▼

EVIDENCE

In the 1936 Munich Olympics,
Jessie Owens won four gold
medals. The Nazi leader, Adolf
Hitler, was very upset that a
black athlete had done so well.

Leisure

Over the years, black Americans have given a great deal to American culture. They have taken part in films, sport, music and the arts, alongside white Americans. American football and baseball teams are full of black players. Some of them are national heroes. At Olympic games in the past, black athletes, like Carl Lewis and Ed Moses, have won many gold medals for their country.

Black American musicians, from Duke Ellington to modern pop stars, like Diana Ross, are world-famous. Black American film stars, such as Richard Prior and Eddie Murphy, are well known inside and outside America. All these people have helped bring blacks and whites together.

But, to many black Americans, it does not seem fair that blacks have given so much to America and yet, in some cases, they are still treated unfairly. Black writers, like James Baldwin and Alice Walker, and artists, such as Richmond Barthé, have depicted their own special black American culture. They want black Americans to think more about, and respect, their African heritage. Such writers, artists and musicians want black people to enjoy the same civil rights as white people.

Eddie Murphy, star of 'Beverly Hills Cop', is one in a long line of successful black actors. In 1964 Sidney Poitier was the first black American to win an Oscar.

At the Mexico Olympics in 1968, two black medal-winners held up their arms in a salute to Black Power, while the American national anthem was playing. Millions of people all over the world saw their protest against the unfair treatment of their fellow blacks.

Black sculptor, Richmond Barthé, was born in Mississippi in 1901. He has made many famous sculptures, like 'Shoeshine Boy' and 'The Boxer'. His work inspired many black artists who began, in the 1960s when the civil rights movement was at its strongest, to explore the subject of 'négritude' — that is, what it means to be black.

So many of the subjects for art are fair-skinned. Why is this, do you think? Does it stop people from seeing dark-skinned people as beautiful? Black can be beautiful too.

Carl in trouble

'Your honour,' said Mr Stevens, 'this is a clear case of mistaken identity. While this young man has admitted that he was seen with known criminals, he has not broken the law. These criminals live in his neighbourhood, your honour, and it is very hard for any young person living in an area where there is so much poverty and crime to avoid such types. In any case Carl has decided that he must leave his home and find a job.'

'I agree with you, Mr Stevens, that the police have been wrong on this occasion. Carl will do well to avoid contact with criminals in the future,' said the judge. 'Young man, I do not want to see you in my court again. You may go free. Case dismissed.' 'All rise!' the court clerk called, and the judge left the courtroom. Carl looked across at his mother, Bessie Mae, and gave a deep sigh of relief.

Carl, his mother, and Mr Stevens, Carl's uncle, walked out of the courthouse and across the road to a park. They sat down on a bench. 'You got mixed up with a bad crowd, Carl. You need to stand up for yourself. You let yourself be pushed around too easily,' said his uncle. His tone was serious but there was a look of understanding in his eyes. Carl had been mistaken for someone wanted for handling stolen goods and he had been seen talking to people who had been in jail. The problem was that it was a poor neighbourhood and lots of kids he grew up with were in trouble with the police.

'Am I doing the right thing, uncle, joining the army?' asked Carl. 'I think so, Carl. You need a fresh start.

For fun, black youths let off a hydrant. In large cities, it is hard for black youths not to become involved in serious crime.

◀ Blacks often feel they are badly treated by the police. This boy, suspected of rioting, is being hit by a policeman.

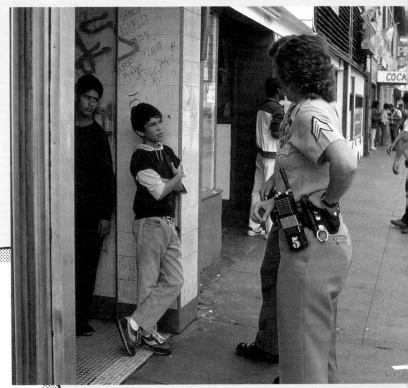

▲ A policewoman chats to two Hispanic boys. She works hard to improve things between police and black and ethnic communities.

You might get a job locally but it won't give you much of a future. Don't you agree, Bessie Mae?' 'Yes, I suppose so. But I will miss you terribly, Carl.' 'Don't worry, Carl will be fine,' said Mr Stevens. 'And we'll look after you and Granma.'

Bessie Mae, Carl and Mr Stevens got up from the park bench. 'Let's go straight to the Army Recruitment Office,' said Carl, putting his arm around his mother's shoulders. 'It's time I started doing something for myself.'

Visit to Granma

'Granma!' yelled Dexter, running up the steps to greet his grandmother. 'We've brought you lots of presents and Mum has made you a special cake!' The family had driven over to Granma's house. She was 70 today and Laura and Dexter were bringing her presents.

Granma gave Dex a big hug. The others came into the house and all gave her a kiss and wished her many happy returns of the day. Her eyesight was failing but she was still very active and she had a very sweet tooth – especially for the chocolate fudge cake which Dexter's mother had made.

Granma lived in an old, wooden house in a poor part of the city. Laura's mother had been brought up there.

Granma's other daughter, Bessie Mae, and her grandson, Carl, still lived with her.

'When are you going to come and live with us, Granma?' asked Laura. Her mother had been trying to persuade Granma to move in with them. 'Humph!' grunted Granma. 'You'll not get me out of this house. This has been my home for fifty years and not even the riots have made me give up my home!' 'But Mother, you can have your own room and bathroom in our home,' said Mrs Stevens. 'And you wouldn't have to worry about bricks coming through the window or rubbish being scattered all over the garden.'

'Huh! I put up with the riots, didn't I? I was in the house alone when half the street was on fire and youths were running down the street carrying loot from the corner store. But they didn't want to hurt me. They were just angry at not being treated fairly, and having no decent jobs to work at, or proper homes to live in. It's been tough for the black people in this poor neighbourhood. And besides it's been a good home to me. I've brought up my children in it and I guess I can die in it.' 'Granma,' said Dex, 'You stay here. I like coming to visit you.'

In the 1960s, many blacks were so tired of being badly treated, that they turned to violence. These women lost their home in a fire during a riot. ▶

▲ In the city riots of the 1960s, rioters attacked and looted white-owned property. This man has stolen two televisions from a local shop.

America is often called the land of plenty. But some Americans have very little. In the centre of large cities they live in bad housing. ▶

City life

Some of the poorest people, whites as well as blacks and other minority groups, live in the centre of American cities. This is because housing is usually cheaper there than in the suburbs, and closer to places of work. Since World War One, many thousands of black Americans have moved from the South to northern cities in search of work. They have been forced to live in old, crumbling buildings, often without bathrooms. Housing is an important issue for civil rights groups.

It is also worrying that many blacks are so poor.

In 1960 one in every three blacks lived below the poverty line. Today, the figure for blacks is the same, even though there has been a drop in poverty in the population as a whole.

Crime is another major problem in the cities. Some blacks living in the centre of cities lose their patience and turn to crime because they no longer believe they can get what they want by lawful means. But crime does not help them. It is difficult to know where they can turn for help because the police force is mostly made up of whites who do not always sympathise with the problems facing inner-city blacks.

This black policeman and his family live in a comfortable house in the suburbs. Many black Americans now have good jobs.

Minority groups often worry about the areas where many of them are forced to live, and the bad state of the houses themselves. Where you live decides which school your children go to, what jobs are available to you, and how much of your income is spent on rent. The poorest tend to live in the inner cities where good homes are hard to find.

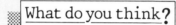
What do you think?

Americans are proud of their country. They believe that it does not matter how much money you have, where you come from or what type of family you were born into. You will still have the same chance to improve your life, or even find fame and fortune, as everyone else.

The Statue of Liberty in New York has, for many years, welcomed newcomers to the USA. The chance to be successful is offered to all.

But the American dream of getting on has not been shared by many non-white groups, especially blacks. Some black people are now successful and well-off, but many are still prevented from sharing this success just because of the colour of their skin. Is this fair?

Patty in New York

'Race you to the mail-box!' yelled Dexter, flying out of the house and down the garden path. Laura was caught completely by surprise. Dexter was half-way to the mail-box before Laura had even reached the steps. The mail-man had just called to deliver the post. 'Just one postcard for you today,' he said, handing it to Dexter.

'We've got a postcard from cousin Patty in New York' shouted Dexter as he ran back up the steps to the house. 'Let's see!' said Laura. 'Look, that's the Statue of Liberty on the front. Mum! Cousin Patty has sent us a postcard.'

Mrs Stevens looked up from her books. 'Let me see what she has to say,' she said, putting out her hand for the card. 'Hi there!' Patty had written: 'I sure do miss you all but I am settling down to my new job. It's very hard work. I'm teaching young Puerto Rican children of five and six years old in a school in a Puerto Rican section of New York. They're great at speaking Spanish – they speak it at home all the time – but it's a struggle helping them to master English. I went on a boat-trip and we went past the Statue of Liberty. How times have changed since they welcomed "the huddled masses" from Europe! Take care, love Patty.'

'What does she mean, Mum, "the huddled masses"?' Dexter wanted to know. 'She means the people who came to America from Europe in the old days – people who were poor and looking for jobs,' Mrs Stevens explained. 'Now America is less keen to let in so many people.

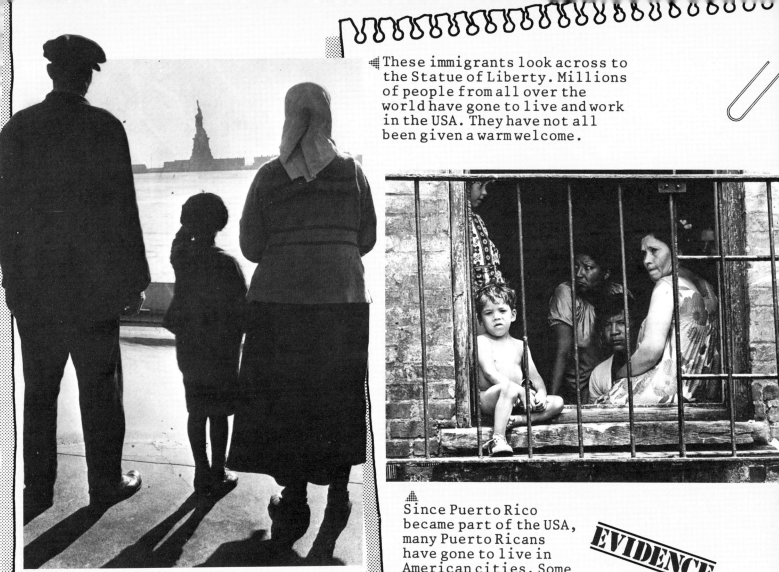

These immigrants look across to the Statue of Liberty. Millions of people from all over the world have gone to live and work in the USA. They have not all been given a warm welcome.

Since Puerto Rico became part of the USA, many Puerto Ricans have gone to live in American cities. Some are very poor.

EVIDENCE

In the 1980s, it is more difficult for young blacks to find work than whites. Here are some unemployed blacks queueing to collect their 'dole' money.

Yet, thousands of people come from Puerto Rico to New York City every year. Some of them do very well here. Others don't.'

'Where's Puerto Rico, Mum?' asked Dex. 'It's an island in the Caribbean Sea, near Cuba and Jamaica. It used to belong to Spain. That's why its people speak Spanish. Your cousin is trying to help their children so that they can learn English and maybe teach their parents. Then they can fit in better with other Americans, and find it easier to get jobs.'

'Are things really worse for people coming to live here than they were?' asked Laura. 'In some ways maybe not,' said her mother. 'It's just that there seems to be a huge gap between the welcoming words on the Statue of Liberty and what Americans think about newcomers today.'

Carl gets a job

'Dex, you're dripping ketchup all over the place!' warned Mrs Stevens. Dexter was biting hungrily into a hamburger at the station restaurant. Carl was leaving for the army training camp at Fort Benning, and the family had come to see him off.

Aunt Bessie Mae, Carl's mother, was fussing and removing specks of fluff from his jacket. 'Have you got your toothbrush, Carl?' 'Yes, Mum. You know you packed it.' 'I'm just making sure, son. I don't want to have to send you all the things you left behind,' she said, wiping a tear away. She felt sad that Carl was leaving home. She had come to depend on him since his father had left home. Now she would be alone with Granma.

'Don't worry, Bessie Mae,' said Mr Stevens. 'Carl's doing the right thing. He's better off in the army than kicking around here. And it's not like it used to be. The army has changed. He won't be washing floors or peeling potatoes all day long!'

'That's right,' said Mrs Stevens. 'It's not like in Papa's time when the black soldiers were kept in separate huts and did all the worst jobs. I can remember him complaining that black soldiers risked their lives for their country in all parts of the world and yet, they were not treated fairly back at home. But it's different now. If Carl does well, he'll get promoted. Why, he could become a general if he wanted to!'

'Mum, you won't recognize me when I come home on leave. I'll be so fit after all the hard training.

I'll have to buy lots of new clothes because these won't fit me any more!' said Carl, trying to cheer Bessie Mae up.

There was an announcement over the loudspeakers: 'The bus for Columbus is now ready to board.' 'That's your bus, Carl!' said Bessie Mae.

Mr Stevens grabbed Carl's kit bag and they walked over to the bus. Carl gave everyone a hug. 'All the best, Carl.' 'Take care of yourself.' He gave his mother a last big hug and got on to the bus. He waved as the bus swept out of the station. 'Bye everyone!' he yelled.

By the end of the Civil War nearly 200,000 blacks had joined the Union army. They fought in all-black regiments although most of their officers were white. More than 38,000 of them were killed.

This black American soldier was part of an international force in Lebanon in 1984. He enjoyed better working conditions and pay than black soldiers had ever had before. ▼

EVIDENCE

◀ From 1964-1973, America fought a savage war against North Vietnam. During that war, a higher proportion of black Americans were drafted into the army than whites. A higher proportion of black soldiers were dying in battle too. Civil rights groups were very worried about this.

Employment

Employment is a major civil rights issue because black Americans have always had more difficulty than whites in finding work and, especially, finding the right kinds of work. In the past, blacks in the USA have often only been able to get low-paid and part-time work. Many businesses were owned by whites who refused to employ black people simply because they were black. This is called discrimination. In 1964 the Civil Rights Act made it illegal to discriminate against blacks applying for work. Job opportunities for blacks and other minority groups are now better.

In the past 20 years more blacks have been able to get better-paid work. This is, in part, because of improvements in the schools and more opportunities for college and university education.

But the unemployment rate for black Americans remains twice as high as the rate for whites. It is not yet clear why this is so. Some say that young blacks don't want poorly-paid work any more and choose to stay out of work. Others say that there is less work in the cities, where most blacks live, than in the suburbs. Black Americans themselves feel that racial discrimination is still the main reason why they cannot get work as easily as whites.

 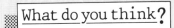

What do you think?

Below are figures showing the unemployment rates for white Americans, Hispanics and blacks. Compare the unemployment figures of the three groups.

What do you notice? Why do you think that the unemployment rate for blacks and for Hispanics is so much worse than that for whites? Is it because minority groups are not so well-educated? Or because they live in inner cities where work is hard to find? Or because some white Americans who own businesses are racist – in other words, they prefer to have white people working for them? It is a difficult question to answer, but the rest of this book may help you to understand why unemployment is worse for minority groups.

For many years in the South, where most black Americans used to live, blacks were kept in a state of semi-slavery. They were known as sharecroppers. They were given small farms on which they had to grow cotton. The landowners made sure that they never made enough money to be able to leave and find better jobs.

Today, black Americans are not always given the lowest-paid jobs. More blacks are going into business or becoming doctors, lawyers and teachers. That is why education is so important: to enable blacks to become qualified for better-paid jobs.

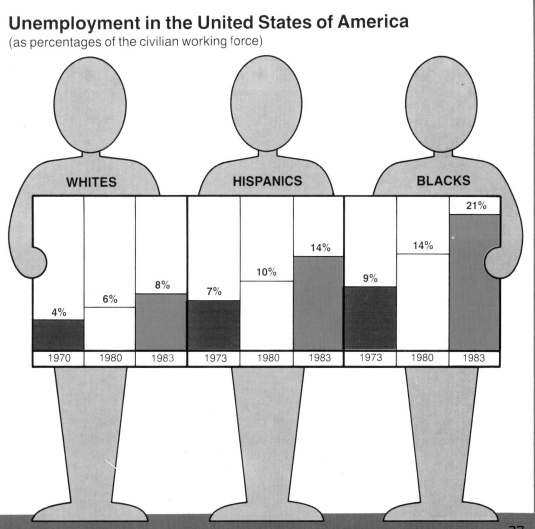

Unemployment in the United States of America
(as percentages of the civilian working force)

WHITES			HISPANICS			BLACKS		
4%	6%	8%	7%	10%	14%	9%	14%	21%
1970	1980	1983	1973	1980	1983	1973	1980	1983

At a barbecue

'You look very good, Mr Stevens. You fit the part exactly!' said Helen. He was wearing an apron and a chef's hat and cooking steaks and sausages on the barbecue. 'Why thank you, Helen,' said Mrs Stevens who was standing nearby. 'How about taking over from me in the kitchen full-time, honey?' she teased her husband. 'I must admit,' he said, 'nobody barbecues steaks as well as I do!'

It was Saturday afternoon and there was a big picnic in the park, enjoyed by crowds of people. It was all part of a campaign to get Winthrop Walker elected as Mayor of the city. He was a black politician and Mr Stevens had supported him in the past. He felt it was important for more black Americans to take up public office and promote the needs of their people.

VOTE FOR

WINTHROP WALKER

FOR MAYOR

VOTE FOR

WINTHROP WALKER

'Laura! Helen!' cried Mrs Stevens. 'Can you make sure there's enough coleslaw on the tables? And if there's anything running short, let me know.' The whole family was involved in the picnic. Even Dexter was running around with paper plates and cups, and Martin was pouring the home-made lemonade.

A fanfare on the trumpet announced the arrival of Winthrop Walker on the platform. He was about to give a speech to his campaign workers and supporters. He held up his hand and the crowd grew quiet. Even Dexter stopped eating for a moment. 'Ladies and gentlemen. Friends,' he began. 'I'd like to thank you all for coming here today and giving me your support. I want to be your mayor because I believe that there is a job to be done in our city.' 'Sure right there is,' someone shouted from the crowd.

'Too many of our children are out of work when they leave school,' continued Winthrop Walker. 'Too much of our public housing is unfit for people to live in. Too many of our schools need repairs and more teachers. I ask you to vote for me. By voting for me you are voting for a better city, and for a better life for black, and white, people!' Great cheers went up, the band began to play and Dexter helped himself to his third hamburger.

Mr Walker walked through the crowds and shook hands. He came up to Mr Stevens. 'How about a piece of steak for your new mayor, Jim?' he said. 'Yes, sir, Mr Mayor! Coming right up!'

More blacks are becoming important politicians. Here, Andrew Young talks to British politician, David Owen. Young was then the US ambassador to the United Nations.

This man is trying to persuade other black Americans to use their vote so that they can have a greater say in national politics.

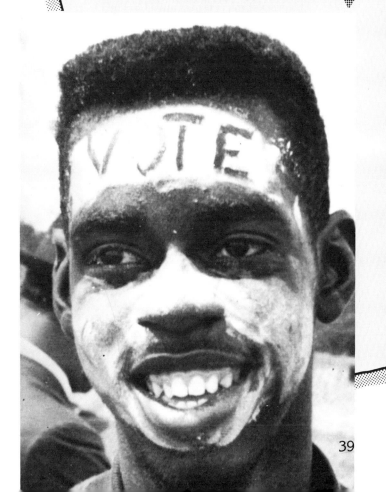

The future

Great strides towards equality have been made in the last thirty years in the USA. Much of the progress has been achieved through the efforts of black organizations which have challenged unfair laws and unfair treatment of black people. The greater pride that black Americans have in themselves and in their heritage means that racism is under attack. More black Americans use their vote than before. More blacks are in positions of authority: more big cities now have black mayors. More blacks have better-paid jobs. More blacks are successful at sport, music and in the arts.

But, in spite of the gains, in spite of new civil rights laws, poverty and unemployment among blacks is still greater than among whites. Schools in the big cities are still racially divided. Racial inequality still exists. Racial discrimination is still practised.

Presidents John Kennedy and Lyndon Johnson supported the civil rights movement. Johnson introduced major civil rights laws to protect the rights of black citizens in the 1960s. But ever since then, American presidents have shown little interest in continuing efforts to achieve equality among all races. That task has once more been left to black, and other minority, leaders.

Martin Luther King in Memphis, 1968, the day before he was shot dead.

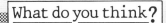

King's death was a
severe blow to the
civil rights movement.
These mourners at his
funeral were proud of
King's efforts to end
racism.

What do you think?

Jesse Jackson worked closely with Martin Luther
King in the 1960s. He is to the left of King as you
look at the photograph opposite. In 1984 he failed
to win the Democratic Party's nomination for
President. He tried to gain the support of other
non-white groups in the population. Do you think
there will ever be a black President of the United
States? Is this the way forward for blacks, to take a
leading part in politics and for black voters to vote
for people who are sympathetic to their needs?
Perhaps it is the only way that black people, and
other non-white groups, will achieve equal civil rights.

Find out more

In this book, we have looked at civil rights. These are the rights of all citizens to be treated equally in various important areas of life: education, jobs, housing and voting. We have found that some American citizens — mostly non-whites — have not been able to enjoy equal civil rights.

For many years, black Americans did not receive the equal protection of the law. They were not allowed, at one time, to sit in the front half of buses. They were prevented from attending schools and colleges with white students, and they were given the lowest-paid jobs and denied promotion.

During the last thirty years, black community leaders have organized a peaceful, nation-wide protest movement to make the government and all the American people see that black Americans were not treated equally and fairly. Slowly things have improved for black people.

But there is still racial discrimination, even today. The government, which is mostly made up of white politicians, often does not listen to the demands of black Americans. One way that black people can improve their lives is by voting for black politicians who will work hard to make sure that blacks, and all minority groups, have equal civil rights.

Things to do

Here are some addresses to help you to find out more about civil rights in the USA.

The National Urban League, 500 East 62nd Street, New York, N.Y. 10021.
They produce an annual publication called 'The State of Black America'.

NAACP (The National Association for the Advancement of Coloured People) 186, Remsen Street, Brooklyn, New York, N.Y. 11201.

The New York Urban Coalition, 1515 Broadway, New York, N.Y. 10036.

In Britain, contact the Commission for Racial Equality, Elliot House, 10-12, Allington Street, London SW1E 5EH.
Tel no: 01-828 7022.
They will be able to help you to find out more about the different customs and cultures in Britain.

Books to read

Most of the books written about civil rights in the USA are for older people. Most general books about America will include sections about civil rights. They will help you to understand more about the country as a whole. Here are some your teacher might help you to find.

Americans, Desmond Wilcox, Delacorte Press, 1978
United States of America, John Bear, Macdonald, 1974 (Easy Reading edition 1977)
A matter of colour: Documentary of the Struggle for Racial Equality in the USA, Lorraine Hansberry (Penguin, 1965)

A useful study, entitled '**Equality and Excellence:** the educational status of black Americans', can be ordered from: College Board Publications, Box 886, New York, N.Y. 10101.

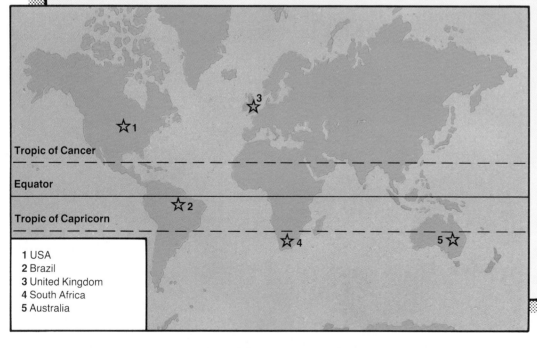

This map of the world shows five countries where groups believe they are unfairly treated: blacks in the USA, Indians in Brazil, blacks in South Africa, Aborigines in Australia, and black people in Britain. Do you know any other countries where groups of people believe they are denied their civil rights?

Tropic of Cancer

Equator

Tropic of Capricorn

1 USA
2 Brazil
3 United Kingdom
4 South Africa
5 Australia

Bishop Desmond Tutu is a leader of the blacks in South Africa in their fight against apartheid. He was awarded the Nobel Peace Prize in 1984. He is angry that scenes like these, of funerals for blacks shot by police, happen so often in South Africa today.

In September 1985 there was a riot in Brixton, London. There were also riots in other English cities. As in the USA, minority groups in Britain are unhappy about what they see as unfair treatment, especially by the police. But, as you will notice in the picture, it is white, as well as black, youths who take violence on to the streets.

43

Time chart

Mid-eighteenth century: blacks, descendants of free African peoples taken by Europeans to the American colonies, are used as slaves.

1861-65 American Civil War. Southern states defeated by North.

1863 Slaves were freed.

1896 Supreme Court decided that it was fair for black children to go to separate schools, so long as they were of equal standard to white schools.

1909 Formation of the National Association for the Advancement of Coloured People (NAACP) – a civil rights organization.

1910 90% of the black population lived in the South.

1915 Revival of the Ku Klux Klan in the South.

1942 Formation of the Congress on Racial Equality (CORE).

1946-48 President Truman appointed committees to look into the problem of civil rights.

1954 Court case, Brown versus Board of Education, overturned 1896 decision on separate but equal facilities.

1956 Montgomery Bus Boycott.

1957 Congress passed its first civil rights act since 1875. Crisis at Little Rock, Arkansas as Southern states defy desegregation laws.

1960 Arrest of Martin Luther King for sit-in action; election of John Kennedy as President of the United States.

1961 CORE sent Freedom Riders into the South to test the desegregation laws on transport between states.

1963 Civil Rights march on Washington – Martin Luther King's 'I have a dream' speech.

1965 Malcolm X, black Muslim leader, was assassinated.

1965 50% of black population live in South.

1965-68 Black discontent with slow pace of progress on civil rights led to widespread rioting in Northern cities.

1968 Assassination of Martin Luther King.

1971 Busing introduced.

1976 Operation 'Big Vote' to register black voters.

1984 Jesse Jackson ran for Democratic presidential nomination.

1986 First celebration of new national holiday (Jan. 15) named for Martin Luther King.

Keywords

Apartheid The policy of the white South African government to keep blacks and whites apart.

Black Power A political movement to encourage blacks to vote for black politicians. It is also a cultural movement where blacks take pride in their Afro-American heritage.

Civil Rights The rights of citizens to be protected by their government against unfair treatment.

Desegregation The taking down of racial barriers in all public facilities.

Discrimination (racial) The unfair treatment by one or more persons against another person or group, because they are of another race.

Equality (racial) The belief that members of different races have the same rights and should be given the same chances.

Freedom Riders Black and white students who rode buses in the South to test whether the new desegregation laws were working or not.

Ghetto A run-down area in a city where most of the people who live there belong to one particular racial group.

Heritage Traditions and customs passed down over the centuries.

Integration Acceptance of a minority group by a society as equal members of that society.

Ku Klux Klan An illegal organization, founded after the Civil War, which believes that whites are superior to blacks.

Poverty line A measure of how much people earn which tells us how many poor people there are in the population.

Racism The belief that one race is superior to another.

Segregation When racial groups, like blacks and whites, are forced by law to be separate.

Sharecroppers Tenant farmers who gave part of their crop to the landowner for renting land.

Supreme Court The most important court in America.

Index

Illustrations
Gary Rees/Linda Rogers
Associates: Back cover, 4, 8,
10-11, 14, 16, 20-21, 22-23,
26-27, 28, 32, 34-35, 38
Raymond Turvey: 4-5, 11, 13, 37,
42

Photographs
All Sport: 23B
Associated Press: 17
Barnaby's: 31B
Bettmann Archive: 33TL
BFI: 25T © Paramount Pictures
Black Star: 29BR, 33B
BPCC: 9TL
Camera Press: 11BL, 13T, 15B,
25B, 35B
Joel Gordon: 33TR
S&R Greenhill: 27B, 31T
Robert Harding: cover insert, 17B
Library of Congress, Washington:
19T, 35T
Museum of the City of New York:
15T
New York Daily News: 12
Photosource: 11BR, 23TL, 23TR,
30, 39TR, 41T
Photri: 19B, 34, 41B
Pictorial Press: 21BL
Popperfoto: 17TL, 24
David Redfern: 21T, 21BR
Rex: 43B
Select/Richard Olivier: 42T
Frank Spooner/Gamma: 43T
Topham: cover, 27T, 36, 39TL,
39B
Washington Post: 29T, 29BL
Wide World: 40
Zefa: 13B, 18L, 26, 37

The publishers would like to thank
Mr Horace Lashley of the
Commission of Racial Equality for
his help in providing addresses of
civil rights organizations in the
USA.